Chinese Li Hua Cats as Pets

The Ultimate Pet Guide for Chinese Li Hua Cats

Chinese Li Hua Cats General Info, Purchasing, Care, Cost, Keeping, Health, Supplies, Food, Breeding and More Included!

By Lolly Brown

Foreword

These cats, held to be a Chinese treasure and revered by many, had only come to the shores of the United States in 2010. The first mention of the Chinese Li Hua dates back to the time of the Chang dynasty, around 1300 BC, making it one of the oldest cat breed native to China.

The Chinese Li Hua is so revered in their native land of China that people are said to actually marry a pair of them with their vows exchanged in mews.

It is a respected cat and is a descendant of the Chinese mountain cat. One of its defining features is its brown mackerel tabby coat which sort of looks like a wildcat. The Chinese Li Hua, also known as the Dragon Li, also has a diamond-shaped head, making them look like they don't have a neck. They have beautiful almond-shaped eyes that come in colours of brown, yellow or green. It is an affectionate feline who loves the company of humans. It is a strong and terrific looking cat. The Dragon Li is friendly toward other cats, dogs and children.

Although these cats have been around for a long time and they have been the subject of or mentioned in many old manuscripts, the first showing of a Li Hua in Beijing did not happen until 2003. They have only recently reached the shore of the United States, making their debut in the country in 2010. It is a naturally occurring cat which makes it a healthy breed. The Dragon Li is a short haired cat that comes in patterns that look like their mountain cat ancestors.

Considered to be the unofficial feline of one of the oldest civilizations of the world, the Chinese Li Hua is believed to have been around for a very long time. Their ancestors have been mentioned countless times in written text. They have probably existed throughout the land for centuries.

They are robust felines. A naturally occurring breed which hasn't been developed through crossbreeding, making them strong felines no major health issues. A fairly recent showing of the centuries-old breed, the Dragon Li, as it is often referred to, has been gracing cat shows in China since 2003 and had only been recently acknowledged and accepted into the Cat Fanciers Association miscellaneous class in February of 2010.

The Chinese Li Hua has a beautiful coat of patterns that make them look like tiny wild cats. They are easy to groom and their maintenance is minimal. Since these are naturally occurring cats they tend to be stronger and healthier than crossbred felines. They are loyal cats who love sharing their love, so let's get to know more about them!

Table of Contents

Introduction 1

Chapter One: Understanding Chinese Li Hua Cats 3

Chapter Two: History and Characteristics of the Chinese Li Hua 7

    Characteristics of Chinese Li Hua 11

        Appearance 12

    Recognition 13

    Introduction to Show Rings 14

Chapter Three: Is the Chinese Li Hua the Right Breed for You? 15

    Pros and Cons of Owning Dragon Li Cats 16

Chapter Four: Keeping Chinese Li Hua as Household Pets 23

    Chinese Li Hua Cats with Children 24

    Keeping with Other Pets 26

    The Li Hua Mao - As It Grows 26

    How Many Of Them Should You Take In? 28

Chapter Five: Tips in Buying Dragon Li Cats 31

    Requirements before Owning or Buying a Dragon Li 32

    Finding a Reputable Chinese Li Hua Breeder 33

    Selecting a Healthy Chinese Li Hua 36

Chapter Six: Requirements and Costs of Keeping Chinese Li Hua Cats 41

Initial Costs 43

    Supplies for Your Cat 47

Monthly Costs 49

Shipping Costs 50

Chapter Seven: Housing and Safety of Your Chinese Li Hua Cat 51

Keeping Your Chinese Li Hua Safe Indoors and Outdoors 52

Toys and Accessories 57

Chapter Eight: Feeding Your Chinese Li Hua Cats 59

Feeding Your Dragon Li: From Kitten to Maturity 60

Feeding Frequency 61

Essential Nutrients 62

Selecting the Right Foods 63

Types of Commercial Cat Foods 64

    Fresh Water 65

    Food Additives 66

Tips in Selecting a High-Quality Cat Food Brand 66

How (Much) To Feed Your Chinese Li Hua 67

Chapter Nine: Good Hygiene for Your Chinese Li Hua Cats 69

Nail Trimming 70

Dental Hygiene 70

Bathing.. 71

Chapter Ten: Guidelines on Socializing Your Chinese Li Hua
Cats.. 73

Socializing Your Pet Dragon Li.. 74

Training Your Dragon Li 75

Handling the Behavior of Your Dragon Li........................ 76

Glossary of Cat Terms 79

Index 87

Photo Credits 91

References 93

Introduction

The Chinese Li Hua is perhaps one of the oldest sorts of domesticated cats that were and are breed naturally. They are adorable, friendly cats who are averse to creating strong bonds with the humans they share home with. They are sweet felines who are truly smart and talented in their own little ways. It is a stunning cat who has a really amiable disposition. It has been mentioned many times over in old manuscripts and has been part of households for as long as they have been around. It is a playful cat with great hunting prowess.

Think about it. People who have existing pets, whether they be of the canine or feline sort, have been welcoming the Chinese Li Hua without issues. With the proper integration process and with a bit of supervision at the beginning, you will see that incorporating a Chinese Li Hua to your furry mix is not at all going to be a challenge, given the proper settings for the meeting. The Chinese Li Hua, also known as the Dragon Li, is an amiable sort of cat with a great big heart for loyalty. There is nothing quite like adding in the Chinese Li Hua to the mix.

All animals, when newly introduced to a mix of other animals and people will need to be given a period of adjustment. If it does seem to be a tad shy at first, don't despair! Given a little time, and a bit of loving supervision, the Chinese Li Hua will soon make friends with everyone in the family. Do not be surprised if they gravitate more toward one or two people in the family. They will tend to do that, most especially if they get to see these individuals more on a daily basis. It is a loyal and openly affectionate feline who develop close bonds with their humans. They are a curious bunch who has a special talent of hunting, so they would be great additions for families who tend to and live on farms.

Chapter One: Understanding Chinese Li Hua Cats

The Dragon Li is a big cat. It is a sturdy one with a striking coat. It has a short and thick brown mackerel tabby coat with its ticked hairs black at the roots, light yellow in the middle and brown at the tip. It is indeed a beautiful feline who has nothing but deep loyalty for the human companions and other animals it shares space with, making them perfect companions for any one. They need only a bit of time to get used to their new surroundings and once they are comfortable, you will see the great traits and characteristics of these cats.

Chapter One: Understanding Chinese Li Hua Cats

The appearance of the Dragon Li is pretty special, since it seems to be a cat that is smiling. There is a special distinction to the Chinese Li Hua because of the distinctive black marks on the upper corners of the cat's mouth. Ok, so it isn't consciously smiling - not that a cat can - but these black markings at the edges of its mouth does make it look like it is. Regardless of whether it is smiling or not, these black markings make them look perpetually content.

It has a diamond-shaped head that is wide. The space between its ears is wide. The head of the Dragon Li gradually tapers toward the chin of the cat, giving it its diamond shape. Because of the size of its head, the cat appears to not have a neck but its head in fact sits on a strong neck. The Dragon Li, like most socialized and domesticated cats are protective and possessive of their human wards. They are keen learners and are easily trained to do tiny little things that not only amuse; they can also be of great help and assistance to their humans. Aside from their great hunting skills, they are highly intelligent little creatures who are able to carry out little tasks that would surprise even the highly skeptical. There has been report of one human companion of the Chinese Li Hua who was trained to fetch the morning paper!

It is a highly intelligent feline who is able to gauge situations which it needs to intervene or avoid. Because of the dangers of street traffic, the possibility of getting carted off by a stranger and the possibility of contracting diseases from other neighborhood or wild animals, it is highly advisable to keep the Dragon Li as an indoor cat when living in the city. This situation shifts to the other spectrum of liberty to the outdoors when living in a farm setting. They are great hunters of smaller animals and rodents that may cause harm and destroy crops, so living on a farm will show their dexterity in the tougher stuff they are made of. If you are living in the city, it is highly advisable to have an outdoor space that is fenced off and high enough that the cat does not attempt to scale it and get out of your premises.

Just like most cats, the Dragon Li, when resting can be found in high places. On the other hand, they can also gravitate toward places that are snug and tight, like an open shoe box or a paper bag. Other places that the Chinese Li Hua enjoys hanging about is anywhere where you are. They will shadow their owners and may try to vocalize and get into the situation of telling you how to do something. This is a feline who takes lively interest in all things you do when you are in their presences. They will keep you in great company, often "speaking out" and vocalizing their inner musings to you.

There is nothing more that Chinese Li Hua loves than being around its humans than being showered with attention and affection by its humans. They love that they are given the time and loving they so need and give freely. They adore the quiet times when they can sit quietly beside you as you go about your desk or paperwork. They live for the pockets of moments when you have your guard down and are relaxed enough to be truly engaged and interactive with them.

Chapter Two: History and Characteristics of the Chinese Li Hua

Once you get a load of the Chinese Li Hua, you will understand why it is such a magnificent cat with awesome traits and possess the behaviors a cat lover looks for in cats. These cats, for the length of time they have been in occurrence in their native China, are few in numbers here in the United States. It is reported that there are currently about four Dragon Li cats in the US. However, other reports have stated that the four have multiplied to about 70+ cats scattered throughout the country. This Chinese domestic breed of feline is said to come from the dynastic culture of ancient Chinese folklore. Dragon Li cats are believed to be a naturally occurring breed, which means they are a single breed. They are not a combination of multiple different breeds.

Chapter Two: History and Characteristics of Chinese Li Hua

The strikingly beautiful cat is known by many different names, as you may have noticed from the onset of this reading. The Chinese Li Hua, the common name of the cat here on the shores of the United States, is locally known in China as the Dragon LI. It is also known as the Li Hua Mau or Li Hua Mao or just the simplified Li Mao. It has been a cat that has flanked the sides of humans and has shared household with us for a long, long time. Documentation of them being present in ancient households in China is many. They are believed to be one of the oldest domesticated breeds and a breed that has not been interfered with by man. It is a loyal feline sort who possesses great quality traits of a home companion and pet.

Indeed, the Chinese Li Hua as whole share particular genetic characteristics but you will notice their subtle differences in personality as you start getting to know each individual Dragon Li. When you do, you will realize how, much like people, these cats have diverse moods and personalities from each other. It is a very inquisitive cat, being the hunter that it is who may tend to shadow and follow you around the house as you goes about the chores of your day.

Pay mind where you step because the Chinese Li Hua may just be relaxing under foot. They could also just be a step behind you, so watch it, should you have to retrace your steps, lest you trip on the cat.

Chapter Two: History and Characteristics of Chinese Li Hua

The Li Hua, for all its adoration of the humans it shares space with, is a pretty independent cat. There are so many reasons why cat aficionados should have a Li Hua in their mix. It is a self - sufficient cat who needs very little grooming maintenance, apart from the monthly nail trimming and bi weekly fur brushing. Grooming it on a daily basis may be as simple as cleaning out its ears and fur with a damp cloth. There is very little need to give the Li Hua a weekly bath because it does have short hair. All they really need is a routine good once-over of their body, paying mind to cleaning the insides of their ears, and they are good to go.

The Chinese Li Hua is known for its superior intelligence, and there are many manuscripts of old which can attest to this fact. There are even some texts that talk of a mystical Li Hua who was able to speak and give bidding to its human wards. A magical creature it is indeed! In real life, the Dragon Li Hua has been reported to be such a highly intelligent creature that one owner was able to teach it to fetch the morning paper! It is exceptionally easier to train the Li Hua to do tricks than it is to train most other feline breeds. The Li Hua has a perspicuous, stark and effective relationship with its human wards.

It may not be the overly affectionate type who would love to sit quietly on your lap, but it does enjoy being in your company along with the rest of the family. Just being around the presence of its humans gives it contentment and makes it a happy camper. Overall, it is a cat that thrives well with other cats and domesticated animals but is one who also loves to spend time on its own. It is not unusual to find your Li Hua starting off thoughtfully into space, not is it unusual to see it in all its playful glory when its favorite humans are present.

There have been a massive amount of reports about the healing qualities cats bring to humans they interact with. Humans who share roof with cats have reported that their tension and stress levels have gone down remarkably ever since they started having their cats around them. Felines in general seem to have a cathartic quality about them that helps relieve the tension of people. The Chinese Li Hua make for excellent pets for the individual who has to be at the office for most of the day. They are independent and can thrive well on their own without fear of them tearing up the house or developing separation anxiety or distress due to your absence. They are playful and rambunctious, much like other feline sorts, but will be just happy to sit somewhere close to you when you are working at your desk in your home office.

Characteristics of Chinese Li Hua

All potential pet owners should take the time to get to know their intended pets before they actually go out and start the acquisition process of taking home one. Whether the pet be of the water, land, cold-blooded or furry sort, getting to know the general traits of the pet you intend to bring home, puts you at an advantage of being able to care for them properly. Getting off on the right foot with your intended pet, whether it be your first pet or an addition you wish you add to the mix, allows for better integration and home transition for the new pet (as well as for the existing ones, if you have them). This cat, much like other cats needs to be watched in terms of weight gain and over eating. The lithe and active is a moderately active cat, with great hunting prowess and possesses endearing qualities which are easy to warm up to.

It has been reported that there are millions of cat aficionados in the United States and in addition to this report, it has been said that there are even more cat owners in America than there are dog owners. This is a great testament to the ongoing consensus of the cat being a great household companion for any individual or family.

The much-mentioned in ancient folklore, the Chinese Li Hua is a pretty big cat, weighing in at 8 to 12 lbs. upon maturity. The Dragon Li is a predominantly brown and black tabby cat with big, rounded eyes that comes in shades of yellow, brown, or the preferred, green.

Appearance

This breed is distinctively marked with black rings around its tail and legs and it also has a black necklace around its neck. The tip of its tail is a solid color of black and on its belly shows a combination of brown and yellow markings. The ticked hairs of the Chinese Li Hua are black at the roots, light yellow toward the middle and brown at the ends. The Dragon Li also has distinct markings on its face and its belly. Black lines trail from its eyes and curves down to below the cat's mouth.

The Chinese Li Hua has two black markings on the upper corners of its mouth which makes it appear to be perpetually smiling. On the belly of the Chinese Li Hua there you will find a combination of leopard like spots, two showing vertical and four showing horizontal. The Dragon Li's ears look like those of a Bobcat, medium in size with a pointed tip. The Li Hua has a robustly, wide, muscular body with a slightly shorter tail. The Chinese Li Hua matures at a slow rate. It may take anywhere up to three years until the feline from China reaches its full size.

Recognition

It took quite a long while for Cat Fanciers Association to get wind of the Chinese Li Hua and take notice of the wild-looking cat with the friendly and calm demeanor. The Chinese Li was given recognition by the association, classifying it under the miscellaneous category. The feline, who is known by different names like, Li Hua Mau, Li Hua Mao, Li Mao, has a cobby body type that is robust and sturdy. Its coat type that is short is silky and straight and colour patterns with an undercoat. It sheds very little and is largely grouped as a hypoallergenic cat. It weighs in at about 8 to 11 pounds upon maturity. It takes a while for the Chinese Li Hua to reach maturity - a good three years of kitten hood glory! And it has a lifespan of about 15 years. The Dragon Li rarely vocalizes, has a moderate activity level paired with a very high intelligence. Make sure that you have a lot of toys that will keep it physically and mentally engaging because it enjoys play time like a boss.

Introduction to Show Rings

The Dragon Li is a fairly new breed that came into the United States from China in 2003. Many cat lovers believe that the beautiful Chinese Li Hua is a sub - species of the self-domesticated Chinese Mountain Cat (*Felis silvestris bieti*). Back then, with the widespread occurrence of the cat in China, the felines were tasked to secure planted crops and grains. It was up to these proven hunters to catch feral mice and rats that would've caused destruction to the fields. They have been referenced time and again in ancient documents and manuscripts, giving credence to the belief that they were originally sired and birthed by wild mountain cats. However, this theory is still under debate to this day. On the other hand, the theory has never been scientifically disproven.

The Dragon Li was initially put on show in 2003 as an experimental breed in Beijing, China. It was given its long overdue welcome into the ring of cat fanciers through a show organized by the Cat Aficionado Association. It was only in Feb 0f 2010 when the cat was given official recognition in the USA by the Cat Fanciers Association. They are still pretty uncommon in these parts and North America. It is said that there are no more than 10 of these cats in the US now.

Chapter Three: Is the Chinese Li Hua the Right Breed for You?

The Dragon Li is a robust feline in comparison to other cat breeds, pedigree or otherwise. They are prone to very few conditions that can either be avoided, or managed through proper care and nurturing.

Given that they are provided with the proper care, nourishment and set up at conditions suitable for wellbeing, the Dragon Li is a very sturdy cat which is not prone to illnesses most cats are. This is largely due to their natural occurrence and the absence of breeding interference. Little will be required of you in terms of grooming because of its short hair. Routine nail trimming will be required and the provision of scratching posts is highly recommended for the cats to be able to file down their nails themselves.

The Chinese Li Hua gets along well with other domesticated and well-socialized animals. It will not be advisable to add one if you have hamsters or mice as pets, because of their natural traits of being hunters of rodents. They integrate well with a household of children who have been taught how to handle and treat animals well. Keep in mind to teach young children how to treat felines with respect.

Pros and Cons of Owning Dragon Li Cats

The Chinese Li Hua is known to be one of the healthiest of felines amongst many, if not most cat sorts. While it is true that all cats are prone to developing health problems, just as easily as a human would inherit a disease, the Chinese Li Hua is spared from many of the genetic abnormalities that come along with crossbreeding. An upstanding breeder would never claim that any cat under their care is free of genetic or health problems. You will not want to do business with anyone who professes otherwise.

Chapter Three: Is the Chinese Li Hua the Right Breed for You?

The first con about owning a Chinese Li Hua is the difficulty of finding one easily. Because of its rarity in the United States, you will first have to go about the business seeking out an upstanding Dragon Li breeder. Once you do locate a reputable and recently successful breeder of this cat sort, you will also have to expect to be put on a waiting list, lasting anywhere from half a year to a year.

This is one of the cat breeds lauded for its high intelligence level. They are highly in tune with their surroundings and sensitive to the moods of its owners as well as the environment they move in making them great companions. They are great assets of controlling pest infestation since they are great hunters of small rodents. It is a great cat companion on its own, with another of the same sort or with other socially adjusted animals.

Hypertrophic cardiomyopathy (HCM) is a typical form of heart disease seen in cats. This heart disease causes hypertrophy, a thickening of the heart muscle. A vet would be able to confirm this by ordering an echocardiogram which can confirm if a feline has HCM.

You will want to eliminate breeders who claim to have HCM-free kittens in their breed from your list. No one can attest to any sort of guarantee that the felines they have will never develop this heart condition. Any cat that resulted from breeding has to be examined and checked for HCM.

Any cat that is found to be associated with HCM in any way has to be removed from future breeding programs. It will be up to you to ask the right questions that the breeding pair, or the parents of the kitten you will be taking in have both been tested for HCM and cleared of it. Make certain that these claims are supported by documentation.

No matter what sort of pet you decide to take in, making sure that you know about any possible illnesses that the animal may have tendency to acquire, allows you to have a better advantage of taking care of the animal and avoiding anything that may cause it to get sick. Getting the proper information about the history of your Chinese Li Hua prior to bringing them home will save you from getting unexpected surprises. Knowing what to expect and how to care for your Dragon Li will allow you to set reasonable expectations for when you bring home your new feline companions. Put this business of getting to know the characteristics, traits and the health of the Chinese Li Hua at the onset of your decision to take in one will be important to your success in raising the cat correctly.

The Li Hua is a very self - sufficient cat who is happy to share company with other pets of the family but it is also a cat that will do well even when kept on its own. It enjoys a certain amount of space and independence and will likely go off on its own once in a while. Although, they are good players! They will enjoy quality time playing with you and the toys you provide it with.

You will, normally, have quite a bit of networking, asking questions and studying up about the animal you wish to take in. This helps to empower your to understand everything you would need to know about the background of the cat. From the history, breeding methods and any possible medical conditions the animal may be prone.

The Chinese Li Hua is a robust cat with very little health problems. With the proper care and mindful maintenance, you will be able to successfully live in bliss with your own Li Hua. Make sure to have a reputable vet in your team. You will never know when you will need to consult one, so it is best to get in touch with one before you actually bring home your new pet. It not only covers you for eventualities of the cat needing medical care, it also allows you to know what is expected of you.

Once you have made the necessary research on the sort of cat pet you intend on bringing home (as you are doing now) and before you even start making arrangements to take home your intended, you will need to start making preparations for its eventual homecoming. You will want to shop around for the sundries, equipment and grooming tools for your new addition. You will also want to check out cat toys to keep your curious and intelligent Chinese Li Hua occupied, stimulated and engaged.

Although a very independent feline, and even though it is ok on its own, the Chinese Li Hua will enjoy it days even more if you gave it the company of another cat, especially if you are the sort who is kept away from socializing with them for extended periods. The beauty of keeping these beautiful cats from China is that they are pretty independent. Therefore they are not the needy sort of cat who will demand your attention. Make sure that when you are in the house, you spend lots of quality time with your cats, playing and interacting with them.

Ask for vet recommendations from friends and community members who have pets. It is even before you get your pet, you will want to consult with a trusted vet in your locale to find out more about the pet you intend to take in. The vet will you consult with will be an important resource of information. They are the best point person to ask about the health and possible conditions your pet may acquire. They are the best people who will be able to give you advice on what sort of nutrition your new Chinese Li Hua will need. They will also be the best candidates to identify illness or malaise in the animal. Make sure that you have a trusted vet on your speed dial.

Chapter Three: Is the Chinese Li Hua the Right Breed for You?

The superbly intelligent feline from China is a playful breed with a notably high level of intelligence and of moderate activity. The Chinese Li Hua isn't the sort of cat that would go into overdrive when it gets excited, saving you from having to deal with an overly hyperactive cat mate. This is one cat who knows how to have fun and is one heck of a great playmate.

Chapter Three: Is the Chinese Li Hua the Right Breed for You?

Chapter Four: Keeping Chinese Li Hua as Household Pets

Pets have long been a great big part of people's lives. They have flanked the sides of humans for as long as evidence of the history of pets and humans allow. Children who are taught the proper ways of caring for a pet has learnt many valuable life lessons. Children helping to care and raise pets have taught children about individuality, personalities, and life overall.

You will want to supervise any interaction between very young toddlers and your Dragon Li. As your child grows, teach them by example and through instruction on how to handle your Chinese Li Hua. You and the cat will always know when it is too much and they may tend to walk away or stay out of reach of people who may handle them a little too clumsily.

Chinese Li Hua Cats with Children

The Dragon Li, just like most felines, appreciates being treated with respect, as they ought to be. If you are a new pet owner, make sure that you are privy to the details of integrating cats into families with little children. Make sure that you teach your children to treat the cat gently and with utmost respect. Owning a Dragon Li kitten is especially fun because it is an amazing little feline, whose eyes is brimming with intelligence. These cats can get along well with cat-friendly dogs and can develop strong bonds with children. It will be hard to resist falling in love with these little purring machines once you get to know them. They are smart felines who not only have one of the most unique appearances. These wild-cat looking felines are some of the gentlest and most loyal of cat sorts.

They are friendly and not at all standoffish. They may not be the "touchy-feely" sort of cat who would invade your immediate personal space, but do not be surprised to turn around and find your Dragon Li in the bathroom with you! It wouldn't be unusual to find your Dragon Li underfoot as you chop up vegetables for dinner. They will go off on their own and explore the house on their lonesome, but will soon find their way back to you. These cats are so smart that spending enough time with you and hearing "command cues". They are easy to teach, not only tricks, like picking up something that they can carry with their tiny mouths, but also maneuver to you. A man in China reportedly was able to teach his Dragon Li to fetch his morning papers! Yes, it is that smart.

You will see that as time passes, both the child and the cat will start to gain confidence in each other, and the cat, to its surroundings. Proper instruction and integration methods will help them develop trust toward each other. You will discover that it may sometimes be hard to tear them apart, like when the child needs to go to school. Again, these are valuable life lessons learnt, courtesy of you having a pet at home. They definitely love pets who adore nothing more than to spend time in your presence.

Teach your kids responsibility and monitor times when they take on some of the tasks needed to be carried out by a pet owner. You can designate feeding time of the pets to your little children as you help them with feeding portions. Your children will grow up understanding the importance of extending caring love to others, not to mention, the importance of proper nutrition and nourishment.

Get the family into the program of understanding how they should handle and interact with the Dragon Li and you will all surely benefit by winning its friendship, love and loyalty.

Keeping with Other Pets

The Chinese Li Hua is open and accepting of other pets and this includes cat-friendly canines. So long as your Chinese Li Huas are not menaced, chased or harassed by your canines, they will be alright. Canines who have been socialized to felines are the most suitable canine companions for this sort. It is highly recommended that introduction of pets be carried out in a slow and controlled environment. An ideal situation to introduce them to one another with be to have another caregiver present; numbers ensure they are given time to get used to each other; also by giving them enough time, room and space to learn to get along.

The Li Hua Mao - As It Grows

Getting to know the Dragon Li Hua a little more every day, makes you appreciate its traits, characteristics, personal individuality talents and skills even more. It is a brisk and lively cat that is reputed to be friendly as it is intelligent. It is generally known to have a gentle disposition. Because of the loyalty it feels toward the family it is in, it shows fierce loyalty to their human wards, acting as their caretakers. The Dragon Li has been noted to display a good memory and an impressive analytical nature. This means that it is able to figure things out pretty easily on its own. Given enough training or time to observe, the Dragon Li can learn some pretty awesome tricks, like opening a cupboard door, like a boss.

The Chinese Li Hua is not exactly a hypoallergenic feline, but it does shed far less than your average cat. This is due to the fact that they have no thick undercoat. And because they have a short coat, it makes them much easier to groom them and they shed far less than other long haired cats. Apart from the regular brushing and combing it will need, to keep hairballs at bay, they will only need a monthly trimming of their nails to keep them in check. Damp wipe downs with a damp cloth will be a great way to replace actual baths (which they won't really need unless they get themselves really dirtied up). It is generally a self-sufficient cat who you would only need to groom on occasion since it is typically able to groom itself on its own.

The Dragon Li is in fact the perfect feline pet for any potential pet owner who has never owned a pet before! Its high intelligence level makes it a perfect companion for anyone living solo or with a family. They are self-sufficient and independent enough to be left on their own, but are equally able to thrive in a household with children and other pets. It is a sturdy feline breed with little tendency to inherited maladies. Apart from the usual bi-annual checkups to the vet, they need very little medical monitoring. They are also a suitable feline companion to newbie pet owners because of their self-sufficiency in terms of keeping themselves clean. Train them and see how well they pick up on simple commands and questions.

How Many Of Them Should You Take In?

The answer to this question will come from you. You will need to determine early on how adding a new pet to your mix will affect your finances. Although the Chinese Li Hua is a breed easy to care for, it will still have a bit of an impact on your monthly and annual expenses. Factor in the yearly costs of vet care, vaccinations, as well as food it will consume on an annual basis, and go from there.

We have mentioned the self-sufficiency of the Dragon Li a few times and this is just another positive trait of the cat that will make it easier for you to determine if you should take in more than one of them. They are pretty independent felines, but will appreciate the company of another feline, pet or human with them.

The thing about taking on more than one Dragon Li is the joy of seeing them interact with each other. There is nothing more relaxing than seeing a bunch of them playfully rough-housing in a controlled environment, under your watchful supervision. Not only are feline effective sources of stress relief, they can also be comical little fur-balls who like to show off their smarts by impressively learning "tricks". The level of intelligence of the Dragon Li is such that merely studying you do repeated actions is enough to learn some of these actions.

Chapter Five: Tips in Buying Dragon Li Cats

The first order of business when looking to adopt or take in a Chinese Li Hua is finding a reputable breeder. A reputable breeder would be someone who has had recent success in breeding Dragon Li cats. Dealing with a known, upstanding breeder of a Dragon Li is one way to determine the health conditions of the kitten you will be getting.

Sorting out the business of the future health of the cat heavily relies on how the kitten is started off in the world.

Requirements before Owning or Buying a Dragon Li

The Chinese Li Hua is generally a healthy, hardy and robust cat who has been gifted with the good fortune of outstanding health. However, as a potential new caregiver, you still have to be mindful of where the cat is coming from and more importantly, who bred the cats. If you are taking home a Chinese Li Hua from China, the cat will have to be issued an International Health Certificate from a veterinarian stating that the cat is of sound health and is in good condition to be transported by air.

This form is basically to satisfy airline requirements on flying an animal overseas. This form is not necessary to enter the United States. However some states in America and most airlines require this certificate in order to fly the animal. Apart from this, the airline may also require that the animal had been administered a rabies vaccination before transporting. The rabies vaccine should have been administered 30 days prior to transport.

Unless the cat comes from an area known to be rabies-free, is travelling to a state does not require the rabies vaccination or is under 4 months old, the cat will need to be given a rabies vaccine 30 days prior to shipping it off to you.

There is no quarantine for pets being shipped into the U.S. save for Hawaii and Guam.

You will be required to present the paperwork of the cat/s you are picking up from customs, or may have to fill out a form before taking your cat home. The cat may also be inspected upon arrival and there is a possibility of refusing the feline entry if the feline displays indications of infectious maladies or other ailments.

Upstanding breeders are individuals who would have had the pets certified to be disease-free. These reputable breeders would have the animal's health cleared by a vet specialist. Deal with a breeder who carries out the tasks of satisfying these necessary health certifications. Seek out breeders who will be willing to answer all your questions about the Chinese Li Hua and its history.

Reputable breeders are easily recognized because they too will have important questions to ask the potential new owner. These breeders will ask questions about the family and home the cats will be joining to help them determine if the family and home the cat will be calling home is a home who understands the undertakings of successfully raising a Chinese Li Hua.

Finding a Reputable Chinese Li Hua Breeder

Since finding a Chinese Li Hua in the US is going to be a bit of a task, owing to the fact of their rarity in the country, the Internet is always a good place to start your search. You want to network with other Chinese Li Hua owners and breeders who will be able to point out other owners or breeders near your area. They will also be great resources of experienced knowledge and a good place to share best practices.

Learn to recognize these sites to sift out fly by night breeders from the good ones. You will need to learn to watch out for red flags that would give indication of shady or flowery messages. The Internet may be a good place to start looking for your Chinese Li Hua but it is also rife with undesirables. Be on the lookout for red flags such as the constant availability of kittens, and being subjected to making online credit card payments.

These may sound like convenient and standard payment procedures, but beware, because reputable breeders are almost never associated with these online payment options. Reputable breeders prefer to deal with potential cat guardians personally. They want to be able to share information with the people the kittens will be living with. They too will want to find out what a potential guardian has done in preparation for the new family addition.

Upstanding breeders will also not have constant availability of kittens on wait. Any individual who professes to have constant availability must be running a kitty mill, stay away. You shall have to go through the process of waiting. Breeders of good repute will add you on their waiting list and there will be a period of wait. Dragon Li cats are rare and few in the US and there is a relatively tiny group of people and breeders who breed them.

There is no guarantee that the information we have here will help you to better identify a breeders intentions. Nor can we \ assure you of the good or ill repute of breeders you will be in touch and dealing with. Therefore asking the right questions is equally important when seeking out an honest and ethical breeder.

A good breeder will not hesitate in answering questions about guarantees they can give. You will want to ask what the breeder the kitten later would do should be found to have a serious health condition. You will want to talk about how the kitten was socialized and see how the kittens interact and respond to the breeder, yourself. This will give you an idea of the cat's personality and will give indication to the amount of handling and socialization the litters of kittens have received.

Set expectations and be ready to wait for at least 6 months (sometimes more) for the right kitten to be available. Since they are a rare, breeders may not be as easy to find.

And there is no way to tell if they are in your immediate locale. Use this time to do research further whilst you prepare and outfit your home for the eventual addition of the Chinese Li Hua to your home.

Breeders of good standing will not release kittens to new homes until they are ready to be separated from its mother; this is typically around the 12th to 16th week or when the ittens have weaned off the teat. Expect to wait another 12-16 weeks after the birth of the Li Hua Mao before they can join you. This time can be put to good use by making certain you have covered all bases for the homecoming of your new Li Hua. You may want to check your home and its surroundings making sure it is ready for the new member to join the family ranks.

Selecting a Healthy Chinese Li Hua

These cats are best known as one of the sturdiest, most robust and healthiest of felines in the spectrum of cats. Given the proper conditions and the right sort of care they are able to live an average lifespan of up to 15 years. This means equates in many happy years of loving and loyal companionship with your Chinese Li Hua.

The Dragon Li is indeed a one cat specie that enjoys a healthy life owing their resilience to the fortunate circumstance of natural occurrence.

Since they are a naturally occurring breed, their good genes help decrease the likelihood of genetic abnormalities. Cover your bases and make it a point to only deal with a breeder who has had the cats undergo the proper screening tests before they are handed to you. Breeders of good repute commonly sort out the necessary tests and initial examinations. They would also have had the kittens inoculated before they are handed over to you.

If you are lucky enough to find a breeder in your locale or somewhere near your area of residence, request to visit the breeders facilities. Being allowed to visit a breeder's facilities is an indication of the frankness of the breeders. Being given a guided tour of the facilities allows you to see the conditions in which the cats are housed, yourself. A breeder with nothing to hide (like sanitation and condition of their pet wards) will allow you, not only access to their cat breeding and feline living facilities, they would also include you in the breeding process.

Selecting a healthy kitten begins with the parents. Ask questions about the breeding pair and their history. Find out if they have gone through the proper medical screening examinations. Ask about how the cats are fed, when they are fed. Stick around and watch the felines. You will have to observe the demeanor of each of the mating cats. Are they mild and even tempered? Are they the sort who scares easily? Are they skittish, jumpy and aloof? If they are then they may not be properly socialized and this trait may be passed on to the kittens.

Given the chance to see the breeding pair for yourself will allow you to see not only where the cats are housed, you will be privy to how the cats interact with each other. When the kittens are born, you should try to pay a visit to check out how the mother cat interacts with her new babies. This time with the mother is crucial to building the confidence and future well - being of the kittens. This is when proper socialization and manners are taught to the kittens.

Do not accept a cat whose history is unknown, unless your goal is to rescue on and you are financially, emotionally and mentally prepared for the possible challenges ahead. Never accept a kitten that is younger than 12 weeks because they would not have been weaned off properly from the mother and would not have been properly socialized to other pets and humans. Good breeders will never release a cat earlier than that.

Although there are no guarantees that the kittens will not inherit any conditions the parents may have or get sick, there are visible signs of the kitten's overall health that you will be able to figure out on your own. The kittens must have clear eyes and clean ears. They should display smooth skin with no scars, scabs or bald spots. They must be able to walk and play without hindrance (save for the natural I-haven't-mastered-footing yet). A kitten that has been removed from the rest of the litter is a bad indication and must be asked about.

Chapter Six: Requirements and Costs of Keeping Chinese Li Hua Cats

The Dragon Li is one of the most robust feline breeds to raise and care for. The revered cat from China is one of the most adorable cats who are so easy to live with not only for its independence but also for its sturdy health and strong physical makeup. The cobby - bodied, medium-sized feline with the playful disposition and intelligence is one cat breed who is so easy to get along with and integrate into the family. Having such a strong physical structure, it is not prone to inherited diseases, unlike most cat breeds that have been crossbred.

Given the proper attention and given a conducive living environment, the Chinese Li Hua have been seen to be hardy little animals that enjoy nothing more than being in your presence. It will not be unusual to see them get their noses into things that are occupying your attention to distract you with their adorable cuteness. These cats possess a fun-loving personality. Despite their independence, the Chinese Li Hua will have no problems spending their days in your splendid presence. You will soon get used to them shadowing your movements around the house.

A mature Chinese Li Hua will weigh anywhere between 8 to 12 pounds. This feline sort has been given the long overdue recognition of the CFA and is classified under the miscellaneous category. Aside from being known as the Dragon Li, the name they are known for in the fancy, it is also known as the Chinese Li Hua, the Li Hua Mau, or Li Mao. They possess short, soft, silky fur that is easy to maintain are care for. This cat is highly intelligent, greatly interactive, friendly and loyal. It is independent as it is social and is playful as it loving.

Initial Costs

Let's set your expectations. Since the Dragon Li is newly introduced cat specie in the United States, there are not too many of these adorable cats available in the pet fancy. It will be best for you to start seeking out breeders or caretakers of these felines in order to get the best chances of having one join your ranks soon.

The price of a Chinese Li Hua will greatly depend on where it will be coming from. There are reportedly about 75 Chinese Li Huas scattered around the United States. Since there are very few Li Huas here at home, there is a high likelihood of you waiting from 7 months to a year before you get to enjoy the company of one or two of them. You may also expect to be networking with a breeder from China. If this is your choice of acquisition, you will have to pay much more than if you were buying the cat locally. The going rate of Chinese Li Huas in the United States right now (2018) ranges anywhere from $400 - $900 so don't be taken for a ride.

The prices will also vary depending on the breeder you end up dealing with, and factors to consider here, in terms of finances would be location of feline as well as shipping costs to get the cats safely to your doorstep. Other factors to take into financial account would be the initial inoculations, examinations and procedures (spaying and neutering) of the felines. There are some breeders who would hand over spayed and neutered kittens which would have also had the proper medical screenings done and appropriate vaccination - you have to expect to pay a little more for the extra care to ensure their future health.

Since they are a rare breed to find in the United States there is a good chance that you may have to look for a breeder in China from whom you can purchase a Dragon Li cat. Given the distance and the precious cargo to be transported, you will most likely be looking to spend quite a bit more than you would if you were to buy any other feline within the country. Expect to spend more in shipping costs if you look into getting your Chinese Li Hua from China.

As with all pets, you will also need to consider the recurring costs that you will incur when adding a new family member to the fold. These expenses will include cat food, cat litter, accessories, toys (they will go through them), as well as routine and surprise vet consultations. A healthy cat can rack up a yearly tab of around $400 to $600. This amount doubles, or triples, exponentially when caring for a feline with health issues.

The biggest expenses you will be incurring are during the first year of the kitten. There will be procedures to be carried out like spaying or neutering, there will be inoculations to be administered as well as a microchip which will all need to be supplied and administered. If the individual is a new cat owner then they will have to expect to be spending for supplies that will help start off welcoming your new addition. Some of the first things you will have to purchase would be its litter box, food and drinking bowls as well as toys, to just mention a few.

Reputable breeders of any cat sort will only make the kittens available for their new owners between the 12th and 16th week. This is the period when the kittens would have been given their basic inoculations. This is also the period when the kitten would have reached physical stability and have been given the proper socialization skills that readies them for the world, namely, the family they are to be joining. This would also be the best period for them to weather being air transported, if this is the scenario you are looking at.

We want to cover you and make you aware of any and all possible eventualities as you wait on being paired with a Chinese Li Hua. Because of the rarity of the cat in the United States, you may have to seek for your cat overseas - meaning; you may have to get in touch with a breeder of the Dragon Li in China. Should you be adopting or purchasing overseas, you will have to be aware that the feline will need an International Health Certificate stating the sound health of the cat being shipped to you.

Along with this, a rabies vaccination for the cat will be highly advised. Although not required by the government to enter the country, most airlines will require this before they fly any animal.

The average market price of a pet quality Chinese Li Hua ranges from $400 - $900. This estimated price of purchasing a Dragon Li does not include vaccines or medical tests that are usually included when dealing with a reputable breeder. Dragon Li kittens cared for by a good breeder would have been given their rabies shot and would have been weaned off of its mother naturally. It would also have been given cat-instruction, schooled in feline-manners and human socialization.

Taking in a Chinese Li hua, or any other kitten for that matter, which has not spent the proper amount of time nursing from its mother and being instructed by her, would not only have socialization issues to deal with but may also have health concerns that would later hound the cat. If your intention is to rescue a young or mature Chinese Li Hua from a miserable plight and are aware of the financial and schedule implications on you, then, by all means, bless your heart and we bid you happiness and bliss with your rescue.

If you are in no position to dole out extra cash and can't have too many surprises spending, you best do the proper homework on the cat you will be taking in to give them the best possible quality of life when they join your ranks.

Not having the proper nourishment from its mother would make the kitten highly susceptible to all sorts of diseases. Acquiring a Chinese Li Hua at a cheaper amount may mean that the person who has the cat is getting rid of a sickly cat. You may get stuck with a growing pile of medical bills. Unless you are ready for the responsibility and are actually looking to save a sickly cat, this is something you do not want to happen - make sure that you ask the proper questions and astute in listening to answers.

Supplies for Your Cat

Some breeders will be happy to part with and over little extras to you and your new furry ward. Toys, blankets, feeding dishes, and foods your Dragon Li kitten had used while nursing under their care may be some of the things you will be taking home with you along with your new Chinese Li Hua kitten. A good starter kit indeed! Keep in mind though that if the Chinese Li Hua is being shipped in from a out of the country or from another state, these accessories will have to be counted into the shipping costs.

Here are other things you will have to get and prepare for before you welcome your new friendly Chinese

Li Hua into your home. Prices of these items will largely depend on your taste, as well as the quality of the product. You will also want to confirm the physician fees and vaccinations costs as these are estimates of the actual amounts.

- Bed and blankets: $25 - $75
- Litter: $5 - $35
- Litter Boxes: $15 - $200
- Waste Disposal: $3 - $30
- Filters and deodorants: $4 - $25
- Liners and mats: $2 - $40

- Kitten Food: $15-$30
- Treats: $5 - $15
- Feeders and bowls: $50 - $150
- Collar, Harness and/or Leash: $5 - $20
- Brush: $4 - $50
- Trimmers and Clippers: $6 - $50
- Toys: $1 - $50
- Toy Crate: $10 - $150
- Cat carrier: $25 - $200
- Vaccination for kittens: $50 - $100
- Vet visit: $35 - $50

And since you will be spending countless joyful years with your cat, you are advised to put your money on sturdy well-made equipment and sundries that will last for the long haul. You will also want to get the recommendation of the breeder about the sort of food that you Chinese Li Hua has shown favor to.

Monthly Costs

Take note that expenses will taper off to a comfortable minimum once you have welcomed the cat into your home and you have all settled in each other's company. Spending will be more stable and be more consistent. Granted that you have already provided you Li Hua with all the initial and necessary equipment and needs, you can expect your monthly expenses to be spent on food and treats.

Get your finances sorted out and figure out the monthly care of your Chinese Li Hua so as not to get stuck with paying for expenses your income cannot afford. Here is a quick look at what you should expect to spend each month.

- Kitten Food: $15-$30
- Treats: $5 - $15
- Litter: $5 - $35

- Waste Disposal: $3 - $30
- Filters and deodorants: $4 - $25
- Liners and mats: $2 - $40

Shipping Costs

We have already discussed additional expenses for cats being shipped from out of state or out of the country. Shipping fees for a kitten being brought in from out of state or overseas, will have to be factored into the initial costs of acquisition. This will be a considerable amount, and a varying one, depending on how far away you live from the breeder.

And because of the rarity of the Chinese Li Hua, you may have to get your Chinese Li Hua kitten outside of your home state or country. Shipping one to your door could set you back anywhere from $150-$300, depending on the origins of the cat. There are breeders who would also have to charge shipping crates, vaccinations and health certificates to your account. Make sure that you are aware of everything you will be paying for. To find out about how much actual shipping would cost you, you want to get in touch with shipping and handling company to determine their shipping rates for pets.

Chapter Seven: Housing and Safety of Your Chinese Li Hua Cat

Prepare your home as you wait for the birth of your Chinese Li Hua. Outfit it to welcome and integrate your new addition to your home. No matter what sort of pet an individual decides to take in, there will be some adjustments to be made inside, and around, the home. Take it upon yourself that the home you, your family and pets live in is sound for every member of your brood. Make sure that you prepared secured spaces where your kids and pets can play to afford you some peace of mind. Making these preparations early will save you precious time with an otherwise haphazard living condition.

Keeping Your Chinese Li Hua Safe Indoors and Outdoors

Cats are known to be curious little fur-balls. This trait of the cat has been referenced more than a number of times in songs, poems and prose. Their penchant for mischief, getting themselves in precarious situations and kitten-like playfulness has been written of many times over quotes and sayings. There are so many cat videos floating in cyber world, that it is obvious, cats do rule.

The cobby - bodied Chinese Li Hua is classified as a moderately active cat. They will do what they do on their own accord. Your furry buddy from the mystical land of China is a playful little feline who is also protective, loyal and an amazing companion for newbie owners to experienced cat keepers. They will shadow you around the house and carefully inspect the job you are busy with. They are not typically vocal but may sometimes chime in to give their two cents about how you are going about what you are doing. It is absolutely crucial for you to outfit your home so that your cats are engaged with the right sort of activity.

The Dragon Li is not only a sturdy feline; it is also an eager eater. It will try to get you to feed them more than they are allowed so you will want to set rules and boundaries. Set feeding schedules and stick to them as religiously as possible. Only give the proper portion of food meant for their age. You will have to make sure not to overfeed cats or they will not be living full, active lives they were meant to live.

The Chinese Li HUa is known to be one of the most intelligent of cat breeds. They are so smart that they can be trained to perform tricks or carry out simple tasks, making them engaging house companions. Teach it to fetch a soft toy or train it to pick up a bundle of mail. Call out its name and they may soon realize that it is them you are addressing. Some may even respond! They are so clever that they can even pick up habits and actions their human wards do frequently.

Make it a point that your doors have safety latches that would be difficult for your cat to paw open. Give your Chinese Li Hua and yourself a little time to get to know each other, and you will discover the keen sensibilities and high level of intelligence of this feline.

Have you noticed cats busily munching on plants? Well, they do and they will. So it is vital that you know the sort of plants that are toxic to cats and cross check a list with the plants that are growing in your planter, yard, or land.

Secure your perimeter to keep your cat from roaming in areas where you have not been able to identify the foliage. There is a host of toxic plants that are dangerous to felines when ingested. Some of these plants may even cause death. Even non-poisonous plants can cause vomiting and diarrhea. Avoid the risk sudden illness. Consider replanting away from the areas your cats are allowed to roam or replace the plants with ones that are safe for cats.

Cats are fantastic explorers who have a great need to satisfy their curious nature so keep your valuable little baubles out of sight. Limit the access of your cats to some rooms and store your favorite knick knacks from the general areas where they are cats are allowed because even the calmest kitty; will have a little mischief in them.

Outfit the family room with scratching posts so that your cats do not scratch up your furniture. Rub a little catnip on the post so they gravitate to it when they get the urge to trim their nails. Set out litter boxes in areas away from the general activity area, but easily accessible to where they can do natures business in peace.

Keep all medicines, vitamins, supplements, creams, ointments and pills out of sight and reach of the cats. Cats inquisitive little guys who will play with objects they can toss around maneuver ad chase after. There is a host of human medicine which can pose grave danger to any pet if and when ingested. Minimize this danger by storing all sorts of medication.

String driving a cat crazy is a real thing. Curtain ropes and blind cords are magnets for cats and you can be sure they will take fancy. Keep blind cords and drapery ropes coiled and out of your cats reach. It could find itself in a dangerous situation by getting tangled and unable to free itself. Something you don't want to happen if the cat is left alone in the house for extended periods of time. Reduce the possibility of accidents by removing anything the cat may mistake for toys.

Make it a habit to pull out electric cords from unused sockets. Cats have an attraction to anything that mimics string. Avoid your cat from getting an accidental shock and get some of those commercially produced wire guards to help protect your electronic cords, as well as your cat, from damage and injury.

Make sure you honk your horn before pulling out of the driveway if you have a cat. Aside from large-animal attacks, this reason strengthens the argument as to why cats are better kept indoors, when living in the city.

If you live in the city and your new cat has not been given the time to get to know its surroundings, make sure that you secure doors and windows. Since cats sometimes like to get some alone time in dark, quiet places, make sure that you check the interior tubs of washers and dryers before throwing in the clothes and that the doors of any household machinery is kept shut at all times.

Tablecloths are great curiosities for felines just as as curtains are. Make it a point that you do not leave your cat in places where they may disrupt table placement arrangements and spare your best china from multiplying to shards, and your cat, a nasty tongue-lashing.

If you have more than one Chinese Li Hua living with you, teach it to understand that the kitchen counter or anywhere around the sink are off limits. They are investigative snoopers, able to pick up repeated actions fast. Cover garbage disposal switches lest your cats manage to work their way around switching it on.

Unless you have been able to train your cat or the cat learns to use the toilet as their litter box, keep toilet lids closed. Do not risk your curious kitten from falling into the bowl unattended. This is important to remember if the cat will be left home alone. To avoid cats from drinking from the bowl, which may be laden with chemical cleaners, make sure that you set out fresh bowls of water for your cats.

Keep all uneaten food covered and hidden where the cat won't be able to get to them. Human food can be full of

additives, seasonings and ingredients that are bad for
felines. Avoid your feline from getting sick, and only feed it
cat-appropriate food.

Toys and Accessories

Unless you live on a farm, where your Chinese Li
Hua can exercise its natural instincts of being a rodent
hunter and controller of pests, your Dragon Li will be
spending most of its life indoors, save from the supervised
forays you take it on occasion. You will want to prepare and
get ready the proper equipment, tools, sundries and toys
your cat will need.

Although a relatively independent cat, your Chinese
Li Hua will need to spend quality time with you. If you are
home most days, you will find delight in the companionship
of the Chinese Li Hua. Now, if you are the sort who has to
report for work and will have to leave your cats alone for a
extended period, you will want to invest in a few mechanical
toys to keep your clever Dragon Li engaged and mentally
stimulated.

Check out some of the more innovative inventions to
keep your cats engaged and entertained during their alone
time. Many of these toys engage them mentally and
physically, whilst rewarding them with treats. Bells and

chimes on short strings and which they can reach from a low level can make for hours of fun play.

Shiny, tinkling toys will provide hours of fun whether they are by themselves or, even better, a bunch of them. You can also give them puzzle and reward machines which not only stimulate the cat to think about how to get the reward, these toys also make the feline "work" for the treat which is an ingenious way of stimulating not only the mind but the physical abilities of the Chinese Li Hua.

A laser-light pointer to chase after and follow is an inexpensive toy that is a hit to cats and should be easily available at pet shops. Not only can it create lots of fun for you and your cat, the device can make for a good tool to get in some much needed exercise. A feather or ribbon teaser is another great exercise aid to get your cats moving. Soft balls and squeaky toys are still great play favors for felines, so put out a few of these around the areas where they lounge and play.

Chapter Eight: Feeding Your Chinese Li Hua Cats

Just like people and other pets, the sound health and the maintenance of it follows if given the proper nutrition the cats require. Choose the right foods to feed your cats and make sure that what you feed them meets their nutritional requirements. Remember that the Chinese Li Hua is one sturdy feline breeds and are the least likely to be prone to feline illnesses, therefore making sure that you provide it with the best in quality food simply increases their chances of living a healthy and happy life.

Selecting the proper kinds of foods to feed your cats will be an important factor to its continued good health. Feline guardians these days have a plethora of choices of prime, quality and equally economical foods to feed pets. Study up on what ingredients pet food manufacturers use to make their pet food. Learn to read labels and decode complicated-sounding ingredients in the pet foods before buying. You will have to be aware of the jargons and technical labels manufacturers use to market their products.

Aside from the research you are doing now, ask reputable breeders for their recommendations on the food that worked for their felines. Talk to your pet's health care provider about diet and have them determine the kinds of food which will best work to your cat's advantage.

Feeding Your Dragon Li: From Kitten to Maturity

The Chinese Li Hua is not a finicky cat and its diet is not a demanding one. It does not require anything specific and they do not have unusual needs for proper nutrition. They are hearty eaters who are not picky about food, however you may have to experiment with a few kinds of food before you figure out the sort of food they take a liking to more than others. After all, just like us, cats too will favor some food more over others.

Dragon Li cats are typically happy with any sort of cat food, or specially cooked food you prepare and set out for them and may even ask for a second helping. Even after a good hearty portion, Chinese Li Huas may effectively convince you that they haven't been fed enough. Sometimes they will be vocally open in protestation and beg you for more. Do not give in. Giving in to its imploring mews and begging eyes would encourage them to form a bad habit of overeating which can lead to obesity and a less active lifestyle for the usually active and playful Dragon Li.

Overeating results in obesity. When cats suffer from being overweight, they become prone to bone and joint problems as a result of the excess weight their tiny frame has to carry. This condition can be aggravated, making the cat lead a stoic and stagnant lifestyle. When cats are inactive, they grow bigger. Watch their bones and take care that they do not put on weight they are not meant to have.

Feeding Frequency

The recommended feeding frequency for a kitten is three separate feedings throughout the day until it reaches 7 months old. Past the 7th-month milestone, you should lessen the feeding frequency to two times a day whilst increasing the portion sizes of the feedings. Experienced cat caregivers typically suggest feeding the cat a premium dry cat food that is grain free because the product would have less "fillers" in the mixture. This ensures that only usable nutrients are present in the meals devoid of additives and ingredients that are of no nutritional value to felines.

Grain free, premium dry cat food is a bit more costly than most grocery store brands, but saves you a bit in the long run because it would mean less spending on additional supplements. Your cat benefits health wise in the long run as you enjoy a bit of long term cash savings. Another advantage to choosing premium dry cat food is fewer poops to scoop from your feline's litter box.

Essential Nutrients

Maintenance of the overall good health of your Dragon Li will save you from spending for costly and unexpected health care. Since these cats are blessed with good health, this means you have a greater budget to serve up top quality, tasty food for your loyal furry companion.

Proper provision of optimum dry pet food will essentially supply the cat with all the important nutritional requirements of the Chinese Li Hua. Choose the correct sorts of foods and offer it a variety of healthy food choices.

Providing them with high quality pet food will supply your feline all the vitamins, minerals and nutrients it would need to thrive in good health.

As your Chinese Li Hua matures, lessen the meal frequency from three to two meals each day and add more food to each of the two servings.

Selecting the Right Foods

Some pet food manufacturers would label their products with words like "meals" and "by-products", make it a point to stay away from them because these are made out of questionable animal parts which were not used in the processing of foods meant for people. These meat parts could be an assortment of unusable parts of a cow, pork, or chicken and can be the feet, beak, or legs, tongue, nose, hooves, tail, or ear, of a farm animal. Some manufacturers even mix in roadkill to add volume to their products! Make sure you learn to decipher labels.

A host of additives are usually mixed in to a food batch to mask the inferiority of the food product. Be mindful that many preservatives are also carcinogens to humans which cause cancer. Preservatives, when used to make pet food, limit bacteria growth and inhibit food oxidation. Your pet will not mind how the food you serve appears, only how the food would tastes. Keep in mind that choosing the right kind of food for your pet will be your responsibility.

Stay away from pet food products which contain preservatives like BHT, BHA, sodium nitrate, and nitrate. Some pet food manufacturers use artificial colouring to make the food more appealing and enticing to eat. Bear in mind that these ingredients that give colour to the food have no impactful nutritional values and these ingredients may pose health risks and allergic reactions later.

Types of Commercial Cat Foods

Premium dry cat food is one of the best choices for your feline pet and is highly recommended. These kinds of pet foods not only have a longer shelf life, it also helps clean the teeth of your feline. Premium grade canned food, mixed in with a bit of water, is another food choice which will sustain your cat's nutritional requirements. Canned pet food does not last keep very long once outside the can so this will have to be consumed within a short period of time once set out. Premium grade canned food provides the proper nutrients your feline need.

Discuss alternative ways to feed your Dragon Li kittens and cats with your vet. Home cooked meals is becoming a popular method of feeding pets It may take more time to select, buy and prepare fresh meals at home, but it will do wonders for your pet's health. Home cooked foods and its sound nutritional components are determined by the quality of the ingredients you use. Remember that you will have to measure out specific portions in correct amounts to get the proper nutritional balance for your Dragon Li depending on its age, and weight

Fresh Water

Cats are known to be timid water drinkers. Often, they need to be reminded to take a drink. Cats seem to favor drinking from a source where running water flows, like a fountain, to drinking water from a bowl. Water is a vital component that helps cool down the cat and hydrate itself. Always have fresh water set out for your cats to drink from at any given time of the day and replenish this with fresh water when needed.

Food Additives

Food additives in pet food products should be questioned by a pet owner. If you are a new pet owner, you will have to develop skills to help decode food labels to make sound choices and confidently serve up only the most nutritious food to your feline friends.

There are food additives used to enhance the quality and shelf life of the food. There are others which are utterly unhealthy and only put into the food mix to act as fillers and extenders, giving the food added volume and luster.

Tips in Selecting a High-Quality Cat Food Brand

- Do not be swayed by commercial food hype. Take it upon yourself to learn how to read and figure out the ingredients printed on labels Understand what sort of ingredients go into the pet food you get for your pets.

- Most high-end brands are expensive and will boast of high quality ingredients used in their pet food products. Products labeled as gourmet or premium are not bound to include better quality ingredients in the food they manufacture, than other less costly, balanced and complete pet foods.

- Foods labeled as "natural" have ingredients which are derived only from animal, plant or mined sources. Natural foods cannot be overly processed and should not contain synthetic ingredients like preservatives, artificial flavors, or coloring. There are varied levels of organic food. Whatever percentage a labels announces is the percentage of organic ingredients used in the production of the food.

- Organic pet foods do not use artificial fertilizers or conventional pesticides whilst being grown. These are free of contamination from human or industrial wastes and are not processed through ionizing radiation. There is no food additives added to organic pet foods. Animal meats involved in the manufacture of the pet foods are raised without the use of antibiotics or growth hormones. These animals would have been fed a healthy diet.

How (Much) To Feed Your Chinese Li Hua

You will have to expect to experiment on the kinds of food your Dragon Li will take a liking to at the onset. Take time to read labels. Learn to be a food detective for the sake of the health and wellbeing of your Li Hua Mao.

Get small quantities of various pet food products. Make sure to observe which of the proper foods they prefer. Dragon Lis are hardy eaters. A Dragon Li who does not eat may be ill or at the very least, may not like the food set before them. Be observant.

To avoid food wastage and spoilage, experiment with the amount of food you give to your cat. To do this set out two cups of premium dry cat food in a feeding dish. Offer it to the cat and allot meal times to 30 minutes at a time. The food should be eaten within the thirty minutes. When your cat is done eating, measure the remaining food left in the bowl against the initial two cups of food you originally set out. The result will give you the amount of food your cat can consume each meal time. Repeat this for the next two to three days to get an accurate measurement of food intake your kitten is able to eat.

Lessen the frequency of feeding when your Dragon Li reaches the 7th month mark. An older cat will not have to eat as often as a growing kitten. However, add more food to each meal when feeding frequency is tapered. Pay attention to the amount of the food you set out for the an older kitten to avoid over feeding and food spoilage.

Chapter Nine: Good Hygiene for Your Chinese Li Hua Cats

The Chinese Li Hua is one of the easiest cats to take care of and requires minimal maintenance. It is one of the cleanest cats you will ever get to know. Like most other cat sorts, they too are quite finicky about toilet hygiene. Consistently keep its toilet space spotless and clear out their litter boxes at least twice a day. The Dragon Li is a self-sufficient and self-cleaning cat, making it one of the easiest felines to groom. You will only need to clean out their ears once a week and give their nails a routine trimming> Grooming a Dragon Li is minimal but necessary. Routinely run a comb over its coat and inspect it for any bald spots, scabs, scars, flaky skin or fleas and ticks.

Nail Trimming

Nail trimming is required in order to avert the cat's natural tendency of clawing on furniture. Introduce this nail grooming while your kitten is young so it grows up used to the periodic maintenance. The first trimming should do at a grooming shop or at your vets clinic with you watching how they this is done before you attempt to do this on your own. Find a nail trimming tool Similar to what your groomer or vet has used on the cat.

Always have to cut above the pink of the nail. Cutting too far can cause injury to the cat. This causes profuse bleeding when cut too far into the quick of the nail and may develop an infection. The earlier a feline is exposed to some forms of routine, the higher the likelihood of it showing acceptance and agreeability. Exposing your Dragon Li to regular grooming activities early in its life will allow your cat to be more accepting of these routinary grooming procedures.

Dental Hygiene

Introduce dental hygiene while the Dragon Li is young so that it grows up used to this necessary grooming procedure. Your Chinese Li Hua will need a good mouth cleaning at least four times a month at minimum to help it keep a healthy head of teeth and avoid periodontal diseases.

Introduce teeth cleaning early and be consistent with this mouth cleaning routine. Purchase a toothbrush that will comfortably fit the cat's mouth and make sure that you use toothpaste meant for pets. Human toothpaste should never be used on your Dragon Li cat because these contain toxic ingredients which can affect felines negatively.

Bathing

It is generally unnecessary to bathe your Dragon Li cats unless they get themselves into a messy situation that would deem a bath. You may give them a monthly bath in a tub of warm water and use cleaning agents meant for cats.

Chapter Ten: Guidelines on Socializing Your Chinese Li Hua Cats

By now you have come to see how easy it is to care for and raise a Chinese Li Hua, and you may be super excited to have one join your ranks. Make sure that you get the best out of each other's company and accept each other for the little flaws and faults, nobody, not even the sweet Dragon Li is perfect. There is always a little mischief to be expected from your Chinese Li Huas.

Socializing Your Pet Dragon Li

Once integrated into the family, the Chinese Li Hua develops strong ties with their humans and become sensitive to their human ward's emotions and experiences. They are sympathetic felines who are able to detect, and identify emotions of their humans. It may initially display weariness with its new surroundings. Consider it a natural for anyone introduced to a new environment. They should soon get used to the new surroundings and you adapt to its new home. Once it becomes familiar with its surroundings it will carefully gravitate toward the family members who it deems worthy of their affection and special attention.

They are independent cats who thrive well alone or in a group of animal pets. They tend to make friends with animals that share similar traits with them. They will definitely need your attention and seek your company, so make time for them when you are at home. Repeated and constant rejection may cause the cat to develop anxiety. Not paying them mind may have them develop feelings of insecurity, so, allot time and catch up with your Dragon Lis when you get home. It will be difficult not to, at any rate.

Training Your Dragon Li

Socialize and train your Chinese Li Huas during the early stages of kitten hood to give the kitten the advantage of growing up well-mannered and socially well-rounded. They are one of the smartest feline breeds and are often likened to dogs in terms of their level of ability to learn. They are quick to learn tricks and are able to recognize command words.

With its high level of intelligence the cat will seem to "own" you more than the other way around. Set the tone of who is boss around the house and you should be able to set the pace of the relationship. They are smart cats who may suppose that you are their pet and may try to get their way by directing events around the home. If you do not want to be overpowered by your little fur balls, make sure that you put your foot down and let them know who gives the orders around the house.

Effective training requires instant reward or immediate punishment after an action. Putting off reward or punishment for a later time, totally defeats the purpose of training. The cat will not understand what called for the reward or punishment if it is delayed. Your keen attention and consistency in handing out reward and punishment is vital to effective training.

You can also network with other Chinese Li Hua owners! Ask your vet for tips and recommendations on how to train your cat. Networking with other cat owners will help you find pet trainers for your utterly smart Chinese Li Huas. A good cat trainer is an option available to you if you do not have time to do it yourself. Make time for this important milestone of your Dragon Li as you will, ultimately be the person the cat will be getting its commands from.

Handling the Behavior of Your Dragon Li

Dragon Lis are highly intelligent felines. They are not only self-sufficient, they are also very trainable. The cat owner has to have keen attention and employ consistency during training. These are key factors to successfully correcting any behavioral problems the cat may display.

Be consistent in responding in the same manner each time an undesirable action is carried out by the cat. If the cat does something that is out of the bounds of rules you set you will need to consistently address the same way each time it happens until the cat understands the action is unacceptable.

Call out the cat's name loudly followed by command words like "No!" or "Down!" and loudly clap your hands to deter them from doing further mischief. Use a spray bottle when an unacceptable action is carried out. The first few weeks of integration between cats and humans are important. Make it a point to be present or have an equally responsible adult to be present.

Be sure to reinforce lessons each time with harmless disciplinary measures. They are smart cats and are able to remember, understand and recognize when they have been mischievous. We hope you learn a lot from this book! Have a great time with your Chinese Li Hua cat!

Chapter Ten: Guidelines on Socializing Your Chinese Li Hua Cats

Glossary of Cat Terms

Abundism – Referring to a cat that has markings more prolific than is normal.

Acariasis – A type of mite infection.

ACF – Australian Cat Federation

Affix – A cattery name that follows the cat's registered name; cattery owner, not the breeder of the cat.

Agouti – A type of natural coloring pattern in which individual hairs have bands of light and dark coloring.

Ailurophile – A person who loves cats.

Albino – A type of genetic mutation which results in little to no pigmentation, in the eyes, skin, and coat.

Allbreed – Referring to a show that accepts all breeds or a judge who is qualified to judge all breeds.

Alley Cat – A non-pedigreed cat.

Alter – A desexed cat; a male cat that has been neutered or a female that has been spayed.

Amino Acid – The building blocks of protein; there are 22 types for cats, 11 of which can be synthesized and 11 which must come from the diet (see essential amino acid).

Anestrus – The period between estrus cycles in a female cat.

Any Other Variety (AOV) – A registered cat that doesn't conform to the breed standard.

ASH – American Shorthair, a breed of cat.

Back Cross – A type of breeding in which the offspring is mated back to the parent.

Balance – Referring to the cat's structure; proportional in accordance with the breed standard.

Barring – Describing the tabby's striped markings.

Base Color – The color of the coat.

Bicolor – A cat with patched color and white.

Blaze – A white coloring on the face, usually in the shape of an inverted V.

Bloodline – The pedigree of the cat.

Brindle – A type of coloring, a brownish or tawny coat with streaks of another color.

Castration – The surgical removal of a male cat's testicles.

Cat Show – An event where cats are shown and judged.

Cattery – A registered cat breeder; also, a place where cats may be boarded.

CFA – The Cat Fanciers Association.

Cobby – A compact body type.

Colony – A group of cats living wild outside.

Color Point – A type of coat pattern that is controlled by color point alleles; pigmentation on the tail, legs, face, and ears with an ivory or white coat.

Colostrum – The first milk produced by a lactating female; contains vital nutrients and antibodies.

Conformation – The degree to which a pedigreed cat adheres to the breed standard.

Cross Breed – The offspring produced by mating two distinct breeds.

Dam – The female parent.

Declawing – The surgical removal of the cat's claw and first toe joint.

Developed Breed – A breed that was developed through selective breeding and crossing with established breeds.

Down Hairs – The short, fine hairs closest to the body which keep the cat warm.

DSH – Domestic Shorthair.

Estrus – The reproductive cycle in female cats during which she becomes fertile and receptive to mating.

Fading Kitten Syndrome – Kittens that die within the first two weeks after birth; the cause is generally unknown.

Feral – A wild, untamed cat of domestic descent.

Gestation – Pregnancy; the period during which the fetuses develop in the female's uterus.

Guard Hairs – Coarse, outer hairs on the coat.

Harlequin – A type of coloring in which there are van markings of any color with the addition of small patches of the same color on the legs and body.

Inbreeding – The breeding of related cats within a closed group or breed.

Kibble – Another name for dry cat food.

Lilac – A type of coat color that is pale pinkish-gray.

Line – The pedigree of ancestors; family tree.

Litter – The name given to a group of kittens born at the same time from a single female.

Mask – A type of coloring seen on the face in some breeds.

Matts – Knots or tangles in the cat's fur.

Mittens – White markings on the feet of a cat.

Moggie – Another name for a mixed breed cat.

Mutation – A change in the DNA of a cell.

Muzzle – The nose and jaws of an animal.

Natural Breed – A breed that developed without selective breeding or the assistance of humans.

Neutering – Desexing a male cat.

Open Show – A show in which spectators are allowed to view the judging.

Pads – The thick skin on the bottom of the feet.

Particolor – A type of coloration in which there are markings of two or more distinct colors.

Patched – A type of coloration in which there is any solid color, tabby, or tortoiseshell color plus white.

Pedigree – A purebred cat; the cat's papers showing its family history.

Pet Quality – A cat that is not deemed of high enough standard to be shown or bred.

Piebald – A cat with white patches of fur.

Points – Also color points; markings of contrasting color on the face, ears, legs, and tail.

Pricked – Referring to ears that sit upright.

Purebred – A pedigreed cat.

Queen – An intact female cat.

Roman Nose – A type of nose shape with a bump or arch.

Scruff – The loose skin on the back of a cat's neck.

Selective Breeding – A method of modifying or improving a breed by choosing cats with desirable traits.

Senior – A cat that is more than 5 but less than 7 years old.

Sire – The male parent of a cat.

Solid – Also self; a cat with a single coat color.

Spay – Desexing a female cat.

Stud – An intact male cat.

Tabby – A type of coat pattern consisting of a contrasting color over a ground color.

Tom Cat – An intact male cat.

Tortoiseshell – A type of coat pattern consisting of a mosaic of red or cream and another base color.

Tri-Color – A type of coat pattern consisting of three distinct colors in the coat.

Tuxedo – A black and white cat.

Unaltered – A cat that has not been desexed.

Chapter Ten: Guidelines on Socializing Your Chinese Li Hua Cats

Index

A

amino acid...83
antibodies..85

B

body..85, 86
breed 84, 85, 86, 87, 88
breeder...83, 84
breeding 84, 85, 86, 87

C

Cat Fanciers Association 85
cattery 83
CFA...85
claw 85
coat...83, 84, 85, 86, 88
color...84, 85, 86, 87, 88
cycle 86

D

desexed 83, 88
diet..83
DNA 87
domestic..86

E

ears..85, 87
essential 83

estrus 84

F

face 84, 85, 86, 87
family 86, 87
feet 86, 87
female 83, 84, 85, 86, 88
fertile 86
food 86
fur 86, 87

G

genetic 83

I

infection 83
intact 88

J

judge 83

K

kittens 86

L

lactating 85

M

male 83, 84, 87, 88

markings 83, 84, 86, 87

milk 85

mite 83

mutation 83

N

neutered 83

nose 87, 88

nutrients 85

O

offspring 84, 85

P

pattern 83, 85, 88

pedigree 84, 86

pigmentation 83, 85

protein 83

purebred 87

S

show 83, 87

skin 83, 87, 88

standard 84, 85, 87

T

tail 85, 87

traits 88

Photo Credits

Page 1 Photo by user AndyLeo@Photography via Flickr.com,

https://www.flickr.com/photos/14-24mm/3002716118/

Page 4 Photo by user Anaa Yoo via Flickr.com,

https://www.flickr.com/photos/54844390@N05/5110233061/

Page 9 Photo by user Ole Martin Bjørnli Günther via Flickr.com,

https://www.flickr.com/photos/bjornlifoto/4175365448/

Page 18 Photo by user Cristian Janke via Flickr.com,

https://www.flickr.com/photos/shutdown/2602070336/

Page 25 Photo by user bartlettbee via Flickr.com,

https://www.flickr.com/photos/88534689@N08/8722582077/

Page 34 Photo by user Magda via Flickr.com,

https://www.flickr.com/photos/85571090@N00/3472867267/

Page 43 Photo by user Malingering via Flickr.com,

https://www.flickr.com/photos/malingering/328212708/

Page 54 Photo by user Phliar via Flickr.com,

https://www.flickr.com/photos/phliar/872609781/

References

All about The Dragon Li - Pets4homes.co.uk

https://www.pets4homes.co.uk/pet-advice/all-about-the-dragon-li-cat.html

Breed Characteristics: Chinese Li Hua - Petmapz.com

https://www.petmapz.com/breed/chinese-li-hua-dragon-li/

Breed Introduction: Chinese Li Hua - PerroPet.com

https://www.perropet.com/2017/12/14/breed-introduction-chinese-li-hua-cat/

Chinese Li Hua – Cattime.com

http://cattime.com/cat-breeds/chinese-li-cats#/slide/1

Chinese Li Hua – Catguide.com

http://catguide.com/chinese-li-hua/

Chinese Li Hua - AnimalPlanet.com

https://www.animalplanet.com/tv-shows/cats-101/videos/chinese-li-hua

Chinese Li Hua: Overview – NakedPet UK

https://www.nakedpet.co.uk/breed/chinese-li-hua/

Chinese Li Hua - Petguide.com

http://www.petguide.com/breeds/cat/chinese-li-hua/

Chinese Li Hua (Dragon Li) - Mascotarios.org

https://www.mascotarios.org/en/chinese-li-hua-dragon-li/

Dragon Li – Wikipedia.org

https://en.wikipedia.org/wiki/Dragon_Li

Li Hua – Vetstreet.com

http://www.vetstreet.com/cats/li-hua